# ALTERNATING CURRENTS

## ARNIE GERSTEIN

Hi Kaleb,

Keep writing.
You have much to
express and the talent
and excitement to do it.

love,
Annie

***ALTERNATING CURRENTS***

Copyright © by Arnie Gerstein

LCCN: *2014906488*
ISBN-13: *978-1494719586*
ISBN-10: *1494719584*

COVER PRINT: *Shurle Lee*
COVER DESIGN
& LAYOUT: *Laurel Rivera (www.behance.net/lrivera / laurelrvr@yahoo.com)*

Self Published By: *Arnie Gerstein*

My gratitude to all who nurtured the belief in my spirit so these poems, that have sustained me, could be taken out of hiding and shared with you; for the deep loving relationship with my wife Kerin, the abiding love and wisdom of Judith and George, the community of Heartlight Center and its sacred land, and my beloved friends and family, *thank you.*

*Alternating Currents* is a compilation of poetry from 2002–2014 that reflects the themes of illusion and reality, love and fear-the journey from separation to union. We are all being challenged to probe what seem to be simple questions that can turn one's world upside down. Who am I? Why am I here? What is my life?

Love or fear is the only clear and truthful choice open with which to answer these questions. Fear is kept alive by our resistance to honestly answer the question, what do I really want?

The poetry is an exploratory experience of love through and beyond the veil of fear and apparent separation from one another.

Our hearts cry out more than ever to be free and no longer driven as a leaf by the winds of delusive desires. However separate and isolated, abandoned and unloved we might feel, if we look deeper we have all had a glimpse of the fullness of life. In the darkest night of the soul, our very being is calling out to know what is real, and to wake up to who we really are. We are a radiant light able to love with all our heart, all our soul, and all our might endlessly, no matter what.

If we see life as but a briefly interrupted series of bitter circumstances it will be just that and no more. In reality, our difficulties are an amazing, coherently timed process by which we are being stripped of our self-made fabrications. We may well feel the pain of letting go of the notion that there was something comforting to cling to and gradually realize how freeing and strengthening it is to be who we really are when our ego world is taken apart, brick by brick. What our beliefs and images held out for us left us parched. We want more than self-congratulating compensations or compromises, more than a brief, veneered happiness and relief when things turn out "our way."

May your soul find peace and love. May you discover your true nature as a magnificent and loving spirit in a physical form.

*Two Worlds*

~~~~~~~~~~

Seeing through a squirt hole
after a winter
no one could stop talking about
a tiny green sprout
expands breathless
from a slab of concrete
into the sun of life

and that day in the early warm of spring
a gust from the southern ocean
swirls in a breath of peace
jewels glint in the desert sand

and  Love Is Real

## Axis Turn

A living soul drops into the earth plane
Makes a daring shift, and like some weak turtle
Loses its bearing mistaking land for ocean
Decides what it wants to see
Disguises reality with opinion and judgment
and begins using things and people
to protect the trembling leaf

*Destiny*

~~~~~~~

Every soul perched in a form
Yearns to be free
To ripen and blossom
Less noticed or missed
And cross into the river anew

*Food*

~~~~~~~~

Desire whirls around us
Electrifying our senses
Abandoned dogs filling up
On junk food thrown at them
Get fat and snarl

## Come from the Four Winds
*(Inspired by Eziekel)*

~~~~~~

Come from the four winds O spirit
And breathe upon those dying
By the sword of sadness and despair
That they may live
Love Again
Suck out the juice of life
And never know separation
Fear or emptiness again.

*Silence That Surpasses the Mind*

Few are swept in at once
The mind flees from sudden change
that steals from the feed trough
Of self concern

Silence rises in me lentement
with the crunching of pebbles
under foot as I climb the moss banked
Emerald Path of the Heart

At the hilltop I cannot move
Words escape as fast as they form
a spider in water I wriggle and am stilled
I trim the dying stalks of
Alchemilia and earth hugging
evergreen shoots browning,
and cut away dead branches
in the Barberry bushes without being
poked and needled by their thorny stems

Silence penetrates the layers
of the animal soul that craves and whines
like a feed-me-on-command child

In the quietude  I ascend
an elevator opening to a garden of love
And the sky's mantle of peace
slips over my shoulders like a silk cloak
welcoming the wind in the cypress and pine,
the color and flight of the Chickadee
in the joyful rhythm of Love

## Lifeline

~~~~~~~

Plunge from the cliff
into the snow breeze
Of a misty morning
Be taken without rudder
mast or helmsman
into a rich life-fragrance

Or remain a moth
Fluttering wild
Around a drawing flame
Cloistered from the world

*Night Cry*

~~~~~~

Tall pines moan in the wind
like cats crying out for love
and children in the night
afraid to be alone
Drunk in the conviction
God journeyed from within to without
Abandoning his creation
Marooned island folk
build pleasure kits
of momentary embrace

Trees lament
children cry in the night to awaken
us from the nightmare of a self-made world

## Emerald Light

~~~~~~~~~

I find you in the moist clumps of moss
the wispy leaves of early summer trees
in emerald wind swept meadows
and the iridescent green of a peacock
You are the pulsating light of love
at the heart of creation
inviting form and spirit
to join as one

*Unlearning*

~~~~~~

Look clearly
Into the speculum
At the sparkle of gratefulness
How much the heart is
Unfettered by tears of joy

In one sudden remembrance
Of the rich clarinet tones
Of acts of loving kindness
That no solitary self
Leaping onto the stage
Can curse and frighten away

What pure fragrance
Comes through on the
Breeze of a new day.

*Truth is True*

~~~~~~

Can a lightening bug
Or a fruit fly
Spill its life force
In all directions
Being what it is not
Even for a nanosecond

*Alignment*

~~~~~~~

Cross threading looks as
Easy to avoid as a thread
Finding the eye of a needle
But soon impatience
Begins its slow burn.
Tools fly, blame rules
Like an imperious madman
Taking personally the refusal
Of inanimate objects
To cooperate with an
Absolutely
Unconsecrated mind

## The Delicate Voice of Silence

Clear blue, sky blue
Light breezing in the tree tops
Such quietude erases
Clutter thick concerns
And I glide like a flying free hawk
Sense free and quite reliable
Weightless on the wings of love

'He that dwells in the secret place
Of the most high, shall abide
Under the shadow of the almighty'
We pine for the secret
Inlet of solace
Guard us from
Our unreal thoughts
Beating us down and stealing
Our breath away as we
Seek to have and to get
Release the self
Cut from the tattered
Cloth of mistrust,
Anger and loneliness
Free us from the hunger of the senses
That makes it all seem
So transient
Delight in what is durable
In each other
A pristine loving heart

## Tallness of Silence

A radiant river streams through me
Tall as the walnut trees I stand
Scrolled tight no more
I unfurl like the pinched leaves
Of an Emerald Fern
In the early light of day.

~~~~~~~

There is a certain silence
That releases the prison of self concern.
An ineffable quiet—
Before the emanation of the primal words
Through the geometry of space

And there is a silence in the twirling
Fall of a golden leaf
On a current of wind
Riding us home
Beyond our carved-in world of separation

*Heated Illusions*

~~~~~~~~~

Pushing our way through
Time-worn toys invented
To entertain
Swimming in, breathing in
Rivers of swamp gas
In the midst of heaven on earth
A fine choice invited
To trigger a memory of
Who we are under a disguise
That seems so convincing

## Les Jeux Sont Faits
### (The Die is Cast)

~~~~~~~~~

When spirit has you by the sleeve
it rearranges all the cells in your body
and you become a wide field
cleared of stone and debris
ready to be imprinted anew

A spiral glyph
Of ancient Celtic jewelry

You are a filament of light
Leaving the lie of dark solitude
To enter the bright sky air,
*traceless*

*Imperturbable*

~~~~~~~~

The mind is a wild horse racing
through a wind tunnel of time
chased by the phantoms of thought

That mind is free
that burns without a flicker
in the altar of the heart.
*"The spirit of man is the candle of the Lord."* [1]


[1] *Proverbs 20:27*

*Epiphany*

~~~~~~~

There is a peaceful
silence of love
in a sphere within a sphere
Where every step is a pure tone
untouched by a single afterthought
that removes all trace of self-concern
all slivers, cuts, wounds.
In that deep silence of love
Emerald Light flooded my heart
Some call it the embrace of forgiveness
I call it the touch of the Beloved.

*Liquidity*

~~~~~~~~

Sharp blue skies
In the warm gentle days
of one final slow
golden ripening of summer
One long surrendering kiss of the Beloved

*Mocha*

~~~~~~~

Endlessly she looks
at me with plaintive eyes
I fled orphaned
And in the time before
the first frost
you found me
And the flowers stretched for
warmth in the late, late summer drought
and thirsted no more

## Daily Rebirth

~~~~~~~~

Leaning down
collapsed and numb
I spin into
a downward spiral.

A Humming Bird wings by
vibrating at such a speed
Pain is transfixed

And the glow
Of loving peace
Is all that is

*Love is Everything*

~~~~~~~~

Raucous pirates
seize the ship
work the phones, computers,
even the refrigerators,

The still small voice of the captain
unperturbed, steers on
with patient and ardent love.

*Quiet Mind, Open Heart*

~~~~~~~~~

I see you picking weeds
and me picking weeds

I see you seeing me seeing you.
Seeing me seeing you seeing me

Slanted autumn sun, a light breeze,
chiming the majestic bells
kittens bobbing in and out of the flowers

For a moment we travel
beyond the knots we tie
to see through the crack
of a quickly closing gate
What is Real.

*Choice*

~~~~~~~~

The antique hot iron anvil
burns slow through the portals
arousing your surrender
While the Angel light-feather
Unsingeable, hovers
awaiting your consent
that the gate lock not
be crashed open for you to taste
the artificial sweetener of love

## Moishe Shoev Mayim [1]

~~~~~~~~

Take up the water
from the depth of the well,
from the feeding springs
let it quench your heart
and thirst no more

Come again home
you who hide in shadows
holding back the swell of
sweet, pure water
beneath the imposter-
All those complaining voices
You pretend you are
Pretend we are

[1] Moses the drawer of water

*Water Source*

~~~~~~~~

Once the signal is tripped
from a secret source
No pin-hole is left untouched
by juice from the ripened grape
and the crackling dry
rocks and cliffs are wet
with the water of the Hunzai

No width of ocean
or body pain
can detour the
unquenchable "yes"
find honey in the rock
and life from the desert

*Intention*

~~~~~~~~~

Bread in time stales
and crumbles
gluten or no gluten

Remember when our bread
tasted freshly baked
did not break apart
When our taste buds unspoiled and
free of splintering sadness or anger
whether someone liked us or not,
If we will have or hold onto anything

Slowly we enter a manufractured world
with mirrors of approval
to numb the pain
of separate and alone
Hanging out like birds
perched on a wire
with an all-day-sucker
to silence the aching split
of a torn soul lest it be swept
into the rapture of life

Before the trance began
Before we entered the settlement house

## Death Attracts

Grains of sand blow across
the back of my hand
fluidly, joining, multiplying,
Filling the channels of my skin
to bury me and
fulfill its end
Shifting and
shaping what it touches
If I settle in motionless

## Loving You at the Tenth

~~~~~~~~~~~

Little sprouts
reaching for the sun
blossom endlessly
in a never ending summer

Oh tiny dill sprouts why such
long roots if not to support lanky
stems and keep us from bobbling up
with each new watering.

If we remembered not
the love that brought us together
would we stay buoyant when worry and fear
staged their loud cry

We bend a little
gracefully slip into
a virtual reality suit
to navigate with all our
opinions about
pain and pleasure
likes and dislikes
good and bad
past and present

Call in a troupe of judges and victims
with life denying beliefs, and host
parasites to suck life energy

Is this not the winning ticket
in a best odds lottery to uncover
freedom and love
in a playground of make-believe

*Skyscape*

~~~~~~~~~

Clouds shift
and blend colors
no brush stroke
simulate or words,
sometimes music.
Layer you with
feathered lightness
Veil you in soft vapors
Wisp you to a sublime thinness
hammering concern will
never perturb

*Ants*

Smell of sweet water
draws them up the thin pole.
Endless tribes of trained soldiers
crawl into tiny blossom
shaped windows,
paddle around
absorbing sugar drink
and drown in sweetness

*Futility*

~~~~~~~~

My dog pulls on its leash
and will go no further

No temperature
or length of leash
can snap the current

Love  streams voltage through
feathered strokes of a brush
 or a choked and breathless cry

*Charm*

~~~~~~~~

He can divine
a snake to stand erect
She can draw men in
with a turn of the thigh
They begin to swerve
and are nabbed
for drunk driving.

So many styles
to be untrue to ourselves:
The timbre of a voice,
announcing the cuteness
of a small child,
Telling another joke
Shining a proud accomplishment
Needing to be longed for at all costs
So precisely we adopt
the perfect spell
imitate, mirror, rehearse
and cast ourselves
in hypnotic masks
to keep away or allure
in a world that seems
painfully alone and frightening

## In-Between

There is a space
as familiar as a well fitted glove
A zone creviced
by bitter-warm tears

A cushioned space to
muffle the clear bell of choice
while a warrior lies in wait
to make ready the flight
from the buckling grip of gravity

## In His Image, in His Likeness

~~~~~~

Would we have designed
a Humpty Dumpty who did not
take a fall from the wall

Would we discover love
incorruptible without emerging from
an apparent ship wreck, alone,
wanting to be missed

## Life Scan

Little stones sink to the bottom
truth capsules descend slowly
tied with in-scripted messages
to be decoded later

follow them on a screen
witness the power of a spell
of fear encoded as love

Floaters and sinkers
seek the light to become
buoyant again
when the air of truth
is stronger than the grey
jello of the mind

*Expectations*

~~~~~~~~~

A beggar hungry
for crumbs of love
to put into his sieved sack
spins on a spiral down
into a cellar alone
waiting for a ring tone
*Blessed are the sackers*
*for such as these shall*
*remind you of the agony*
*of seeking to take back*
*what was not freely given*

## Restoration

~~~~~~~~~

I clenched a worn heart
squeezing fear out of love
one dial two positions
separation or union
A dial in hand

Same energy/different motive
*Not so much*
*seeking to be loved*
*as to love*
*to be understood*
*as to understand*
*for it is in giving*
*that we receive*
*it is in dying to (self)*
*that we are reborn*
*to eternal life*


(From the Prayer of St. Francis)

Encrypted in Will
Entwined in Courage
A hidden pearl of Freedom
out of the cushions of comfort
sings me upward
into the gifts of choice

Cloaks and daggers
All the predator prey encrypted
in nature or in nature from us

Incognitos among the coral, the trees,
From the secret of the tree frog
or the Paraguey Viper
gliding through the sand
gently fading to find a resting
place and conceal ambush
play where choice leads
with each entry and exit
the way to be Zusya rather than Moses

*Bird Brains*

~~~~~~~~~

Black Headed Chickadees
converge on the cage feeder
dart at a seed
and butterfly to the nearest tree
Ground feeding Cardinals bob
for the taste of a sunflower shell
or stretch their neck once or twice
for the dangling suet
more skittish than the littlest among us

Glory be to the highest
and the lowest
No pushing for first in line
Amply letting be
while we stand puzzled
at how they pull it off

*On this Cloudy Day*

~~~~~~~~~

Shielding the Emerald Light
I innocently cater
to a squatter
offer free rent
to an imposter
who seems authentically
interested in my well being
Hand a valid entry ticket to
to a swindler with so much trust
not a syllable space remains
where I can stop doubting
Is that me!
Only a finely tuned ear
shall spot the voice of truth
and not so much seek
to accommodate to another
as to fly free that magnetic pull

## The Perfect Arrangement

~~~~~~~~~~

Resistance meets a wave of love
The play of light and shadow begins
Surrender pulls on the tough
School of the America assassin trainer,
holding cards too close to the chest to let go

Love challenges every hold-out
with a well-tailored obstacle
to jar loose the tightest container

Every hoarder of self-importance
survivor in pain-proof armor
flipper of properties

Each pushed to the event horizon
where outside knows not
what's cooking the inside
Until the agony can hold no longer
and the Chrysalis of the heart opens
to release its butterfly

## Universal Magnet

You knocked me down with
a strong hand and outstretched arm
word stinging salt from the sea
driving gusts of wind walking me backward
to keep  from breathing ice into my nostrils

All the clutter of scrap iron drawn
by a magnet out of me
will not release its attraction
until I desire enough to leave
the pulls of my occluded way
that I might hear untying
laces slap my shoes
my breath enters and leaves
Catch a wind my little boat and I
and depart the protective calm
to know worthiness at sea

## Perfect Timing

~~~~~~~~

That long nightly path
through dark stairs
and crumbling tunnels
into the dark, hot furnace cellar
raking away dying clinkers
from the burning coals
piping warmth to the tenants
with fierce immigrant determination

Rabbi, son of a demeaning father
no master of the suave to win over
a congregation or a board of directors.

Exit patterns engraved themselves quickly
jolting him from congregation to
congregation to learn the message, "this is
not for you anymore."

Each day masked by coal soot
bleeded of life, climbed the stairs in pain
and took his seat near the back door
for a warm meal swallowed in gulps

that comforted me in their choked pain
over the non-paying tenants and no-show
workers leaving him to do their work.

All this dry giving, tearing
at his engine piece by piece
stamped him, and he signed
"it's too late for me now,
I can't do it anymore"

Our Americanized Sisyphus
in a rare, pleasurable, climactic moment
of intimacy, signed out
arresting the cry of broken dreams–


*May you wake, dad, to the morning sun*
*walk above the deep furrows*
*dug by the tight expectations of others*
*And from the deep ocean of impeccable choice*
*endlessly recover who you are,*
*what is your life and why you are here.*

## Miracles Happen

~~~~~~~~~

A gentle current of air moves
through the very top branches of the pine
and life breathes in the heart of a woman
slumped lifeless in her wheelchair
at the nursing home

Weak pilgrim, her arm in the air
signaling, 'I am here'
in perfect sync with the moment
a beloved one kneeling beside her
transmits a message
from the secret
place of the most high
"Do not be afraid. You are not alone."

## Miracle of Choice

You glanced at him
from across the aisle
through a one-way mirror
Froze him in a frame
pitched a story line
and constructed one more alien
with each glance of cloaked
disgust and fear

And you met again
in the Baggage Claim area
for a conversion ceremony of
'No' to 'yes' claiming life from
a frozen past
of unmoving images so we
might exchange delightful recipes
for a new soup dé jour each night

## The Moroccan Maid

Rahima compassionate one
called it Sponja and her hips swayed as she
as she danced across the cold tile
with wide sweeps of the rag covered mop
on her knees breathing without strain
Supple movements one room to the next
erasing the gap between work and play
carved into her mind ages since Plato
tried to release us from the cave where
illusion simulates reality

I punch it down and it rises
I am the yeast and the glory
How I rubbed against the grain
and slivered my skin
Let it be done through me
In nerve and fascia
without the flea itch
of anxiety watching the pot boil

*Unflappable*

In an alley of East Jerusalem
the old man siezed
and fell to the ground
eyes rolled up and fluttering
streaming saliva
as silent ticket holders gather at
the appointed time for
for the afternoon showing.
Love's spirit kneels to caress
the lone bird and cradle
its head from banging against
the urine stenched stone

## The Heat is On

~~~~~~~

Cables of the neck tighten
from the winter drag-on
Plows and shovels race
to tame floods of snow and ice
inner rage turns the animal soul
against the wall of  the other
thick with the thought
"spring will never come."

Amnesiacs leaden off
the consenting experiment
to penetrate the veil
of need and want
of burrowed breath
unwilling yet
to inhale deep
into the painless
truth springing from
the knowing heart
and hear bright news flashing
Who you are
Why you are here

*My Will Be Done*

An itch more induced than real
wracked between past and future
"What if' 'why didn't I, 'it is just not
good enough.'
from the tiniest rush to survive
each in our special worlds
dropping away from one another
insulated from the heart of love

'Se parare'
the slow process of preparing
to move apart
to divide the whole
into individual elements
and become separatists
in a playing field-school of the ego
where knives of separation carve
an illusion of need and  lack

and we create legacies to
arrest the sand's run on time
lest we sink into oblivion

Endless lies to barely cover the truth
of our innate goodness

*Out of the Rock*

Stinging bees
defend their honey
in crevices of rocky terrain
where olive trees bear fruit
an emollient to the hardness we endure

When our stiff necks loosen
we reach into the holes
to taste sweet nectar
find love in tightly combed spaces
anoint ourselves with oil of olive
weakened no further
by the shattering illusion of separation

Proof

Made in the USA
Charleston, SC
23 May 2014